Carlo Maria C

DRAWN TO THE LORD

Six stories of vocation
Maximilian Kolbe
Thérèse of the Child Jesus
Charles de Foucauld
Simone Weil
Giorgio La Pira
Robert and Christine

VERITAS

Published 1987 by
Veritas Publications
7-8 Lower Abbey Street
Dublin 1

Italian language edition published 1983 by
Edizioni Paoline
Via Paolo Uccello 9
20148 Milan
Italy

ISBN: 0 86217 248 9

Translation: Patrick Rogers
Cover design: Eddie McManus
Typesetting: Printset & Design Ltd, Dublin
Printed in the Republic of Ireland by
Mount Salus Press Ltd, Dublin

CONTENTS

Christian meditation

is man's dialogue with God
in Christ and in the Spirit

is listening to and then receiving
the Word

is opening one's whole being
to the triune God

is man's co-operation
with the action of God

is the gift of his grace

Preface

We[1] have been requested again this year to publish the talks recorded during Archbishop Martini's meetings with young people in the Cathedral of Milan. We are happy to do so, in the light of the success of the earlier volumes covering the meetings during the years 1980-81 and 1981-82.

Naturally, what was said at these meetings was not originally intended to appear in published form. It does not follow the strict order one might expect in a book, but it is rather the view of the Archbishop speaking to the crowds of young people who gathered to pray along with him. The spoken word is always richer than the written, even though less strictly organised.

The Archbishop's 'School of Prayer' in Milan arose from three years of these meetings, which were an important part of preparing for the twentieth Italian Eucharistic Congress, celebrated in May 1983 and personally attended by Pope John Paul II. The Archbishop himself stressed that these meetings, held on the first Thursday of each month, were a real school which prepared the great popular prayer of the Congress.

The process began in the autumn of 1980, in response to two converging wishes: first, that of the Archbishop himself to open up an experience of living Christian prayer to everyone who is in search of deeper meaning in life; and second, that of some young people in the Catholic Action movement, who wanted to come together for meditation, to reflect and to pray in company with others of their own age, especially those who did not belong to any Christian group, either in their parish or elsewhere.

Someone suggested, 'Why not hold our meetings in the

1. Edizioni Paoline, the publishers of the original Italian language edition.

Cathedral, and invite the Archbishop along?' The meetings began with great enthusiasm and commitment. The contemplative dimension of life, the primacy of the Word and the centrality of the Eucharist are the three themes the Cardinal proposed to explore with the faithful in his diocese. Several 'schools' of meditation had already been held in the Cathedral: The Journey of Prayer with the evangelist Luke, The Problem of God and Man in the Psalms, and Life as Vocation in relation to the Eucharistic Christ who draws all to himself.

The young people attended in ever growing numbers. They felt themselves understood, challenged, helped and loved — and so they kept attending on the first Thursday of every month. It was not only those who belonged to groups like Catholic Action but — as was hoped from the beginning — young people came, often from quite a distance, and those who would not normally be in the habit of going to church. On several occasions the whole Cathedral was packed to bursting point. The Archbishop's friendly manner and the simple yet profound things he had to say helped them reflect on the living meaning of the Bible text and guided them to the prayer of adoration, to silence and to the Eucharist. Little by little the young people found what they were looking for and answers even to questions that they had hardly asked before.

These Thursday meetings were something to talk about afterwards as numbers of these young people took the opportunity to say to disillusioned and sceptical friends at school or at work, 'Come to the cathedral and see for yourself.'

We are grateful both to the Cardinal Archbishop and to those young people from Catholic Action who suggested these meetings. Between them they challenged us to have the *courage* to hold onto the full message of Christ and take our proper place in the march of history, incarnating the Eternal Word in the events of everyday life. They reminded us that we should have more *hope* that our world, under the impulse of the Spirit of God, is really heading towards salvation. Also, that we should have more *generosity* in helping the Church to find the face of Christ who dwells within humanity.

1

LORD, DRAW US TO YOURSELF

First meeting, 3 November 1982

Biblical Text: John 12:20-33

'Among those who went up to worship at the feast were some Greeks. These came to Philip, who was from Bethsaida in Galilee, and said to him, "Sir, we wish to see Jesus." Philip went and told Andrew; Andrew went with Philip and they told Jesus. And Jesus answered them, "The hour has come for the Son of man to be glorified. Truly, truly, I say to you, unless a grain of wheat falls into the earth and dies, it remains alone; but if it dies, it bears much fruit. He who loves his life loses it, and he who hates his life in this world will keep it for eternal life. If any one serves me, he must follow me; and where I am, there shall my servant be also; if any one serves me, the Father will honour him."

Now is my soul troubled. And what shall I say? "Father, save me from this hour"? No, for this purpose I have come to this hour. "Father, glorify thy name." Then a voice came from heaven, "I have glorified it, and I will glorify it again." The crowd standing by heard it and said that it had thundered. Others said, "An angel has spoken to him." Jesus answered, "This voice has come for your sake, not for mine. Now is the judgment of this world, now shall the ruler of this world be cast out; and I, when I am lifted up from the earth, will draw all to myself." He said this to show by what death he was to die.'

Homily

A heartfelt welcome to all of you! I am really happy to be here with you again, and I ask the Lord that our prayer may rise out of a genuine listening to his Word so it can become the gift of his Spirit working in each one of us.

The main theme of our readings and reflections throughout this series of meetings will be: 'I will draw all to myself.' So we begin with the Gospel text where Jesus actually says these words. The sub-title 'Word, Eucharist, Vocation' expresses our desire to show the relationship between these three fundamental realities of Christian experience. We want to explore how the primacy of the Word, the centrality of the Eucharist and our personal vocation in life can all come together into *a unity*.

From our next meeting onward, we will examine some particular aspects of vocation through people who offer the witness of a full and rich existence — four men and three women, whose example suggests ways for better understanding our own lives. After reflecting on their example we will move to some Scripture text which in turn will throw light on some aspect of their lives. Throughout the whole process we will keep in mind the Eucharist as the presence of Christ drawing every life to himself.

This opening meditation is based on chapter twelve of the Gospel of St John, where it says: 'Now is the judgment of this world, now shall the ruler of this world be cast out. And I when I am lifted up from the earth will draw all to myself' (*31-32*). In a book that he wrote in 1850 under the title *A school of Christianity*, the Danish philosopher and spiritual writer, Soren Kierkegaard, made a famous commentary on this gospel text. He devotes no fewer than seven meditations to the Lord's promise: 'I will draw all to myself.' Let me read for you the prayer with which these meditations begin:

'Lord Jesus Christ, the things that hold us back from you are so varied: all those sterile worries, futile pleasures and vain preoccupations. So many things tend to distract or frighten us and make us hold back — pride, which makes us too cowardly to accept help from others — timidity, which draws us back to self-destruction — remorse for past sins, which flees before the purity of what is holy as sickness flees from the doctor's remedy. And yet in spite of all, you are stronger than all.... Draw us to you ever more strongly!

We call you Saviour and Redeemer. You came into this world to set us free from the chains that bind us, even those of our own making, and to save those whom you have redeemed. This is the work you have achieved and will achieve until the end of time. It shall be according to *your* word: Lifted up from the earth, you will draw all to yourself!'

This prayer of Kierkegaard is profoundly liberating because it affirms how it is Jesus himself who draws us, attracts us and awakens each one of us to the mystery of God, hidden within our own selves. I have no other wish in this school of prayer, than to help this mystery to resound in your hearts.

The words of Jesus
These words were among the last spoken by Jesus during his public life. They come within the broader context of chapter twelve of the Gospel of St John: A welcoming crowd of people coming out from Jerusalem waving palm branches; at this point some Greeks ask Philip to be allowed meet Jesus. But our Lord replies with a puzzling phrase: 'If the grain of wheat does not fall to the earth and die, it remains alone.'

Then (the text continues) he appears profoundly disturbed and comes near to asking the Father to set him free from his hour of destiny, because he cannot bear to endure it... and yet he adds: 'But for this I have come. Father, glorify your name.' This is followed by the mysterious comforting voice and then Jesus says out loud: 'Now is the sentence of condemnation against the present order of things and its leader. And I when I am lifted from the earth will draw all to myself.' This gives accurately the meaning of the text.

Let us see if we can understand, first the words that suggest something negative: the *condemnation* of the present order of things; then we will move to the positive promise, *'I will draw all to myself.'*

'The present order of things'
What is meant by 'this order of things', which is usually translated as 'this world'? It is the world as dominated by structures in a negative sense: that is, the whole set of conventions

and conditions that block and impede our personal spirit and life, that of the group, or even that of society as a whole. You might also call it the negative side of the dominant culture; the combination of cynical voices that produce sadness and lack of commitment; the set of pressures that foster the victory of particular interests over the common good; the combined forces that lead to scepticism concerning the prospects of achieving peace and reconciliation. Negative forces like these have deep roots even within ourselves and can stop us committing ourselves to what is positive, fraternal and trustful. Sometimes these are hidden under a mask of harmless frivolity while the underlying reality is an attitude of coldness, insensitivity and selfishness — everything, in fact, which lowers the level of love within each of us and in our world.

This negative order of things has a head: the prince of this world. Jesus wants to tell us something that is difficult to understand and which we can express by saying that there is an evil intelligence in the world. Evil in this world is not simply the combined sum of human folly and mistakes: there is an obvious depth of malice which appears as diabolic manifestations. We need only think of extermination camps, of torture, of those who embrace death in the fatal self-destruction of drugs. These are extreme cases in which a definite evil intelligence confronts us as an actual life-destroying meaninglessness.

Already condemned
However, this order of things is already condemned. And the sentence of condemnation that unmasks it is the death of Christ himself. Jesus on the Cross unmasks this set of inclinations, of selfishness, of insisting on personal privilege contrary to others and to common good — all these negative forces result in the killing of the just man, the death of the defenceless one, the wounding of the body of man and of the world. And we all play our part in this wounding....

But this sentence is not simply an unmasking; the Cross of Jesus also proclaims the defeat of this 'dominant culture'.

'When I am lifted up from the earth'

What is the link between this sentence of condemnation and the raising up of Jesus? To be 'lifted up' is another enigmatic word because in itself it could mean the enthronement of a king, some great monarch who, through the force of arms and through politics, overcomes the force of evil. There is, indeed, always the temptation of political messianism. But Jesus unmasks it by his very words: for him to be lifted up from the earth meant that dreadful penalty of crucifixion.

But as we think of this central mystery of faith we must wonder, how can this dreadful execution win out over the present order of things which is so tied up in selfishness? The answer is that it wins through *attracting*, it wins by that drawing power which the death of Jesus out of pure love exercises on every person, on the world, and on history: 'I will draw all to myself.' If the cross draws us, it is not because of the humiliation and pain it represents. Death was and remains a terrible thing. But this death is completely special: it is the moment of passover, the supreme action of a liberating love; an act of love so deep that it allows us glimpse the limitless love of God for humanity, his pouring himself out, his handing himself over without reserve for me, for you, for every one of us: his self-giving that reaches us through the Eucharist.

The cross, which expresses God's unconditional love for me and for my life, touches me through the Eucharist by the mysterious power of the Holy Spirit, poured out by the Jesus who died and rose again. Indeed, it is the only power able to renew and transform the world. It transforms because it touches the deepest wellsprings of our being, the very dynamism of our desire. Every one of us, indeed, has a profound desire that has no limit. This dynamic force pushes upwards towards what can properly attract it; it reaches towards the sublime where alone it can be completely fulfilled.

It is here that we find the Christian vocation.

The Christian vocation

So we need to contemplate the cross, the Eucharist, and Jesus who draws all to himself. In this way we can understand ourselves in the totality of our desires — which only he can direct — for he makes them unfold gradually, he prompts us to unleash all our capacity for giving until we discover the destiny for which we are made: Thus we come to understand our life both as a response to a call, and as a service.

This evening, in this the first of our meetings, we are invited to adore the cross and to thank Christ Jesus who through his passion and his infinite love *draws us to himself.* We are invited to ask ourselves, 'what is it in me that needs to be overcome, because it is opposed to this attraction of the Eucharist? What in our lives weighs us down or holds us back and prevents our desires from expressing themselves in an authentic way? What hinders me from feeling the attraction of Jesus as something very real, drawing me powerfully?'

We are invited to ask the Lord to let us be transformed by the Eucharist so that we may know to what service he is calling us.

In a little while we shall be silent in prayer: I will pray for you, and I want you also to pray that this mysterious attraction of the cross of Christ may also be alive in me and that I might better understand my calling in the service of God's people.

Perhaps we can make our own the words with which Kierkegaard ends his meditations on the promise of Jesus to draw all to himself:

'But you, you Lord Jesus Christ, we pray you draw us entirely to you. Whether our life is lived quietly in a cabin by the side of a peaceful lake or we are being tested in this struggle with the waves of life upon the unchained ocean, whether it is our ambition to live in peace, or we struggle amid trials and humiliations, draw us, draw us entirely to you:

We pray for all people. We pray for the little baby offered to you by its parents so that you may draw it to yourself. We pray also for those who have renewed their covenant with you after breaking it. We pray for those who have known what gives this earthly life its most beautiful meaning.

We pray for those who find themselves in love, for those who love each other, that they may not promise more to each other than they are able to keep. We pray for the bridegroom and his bride. We pray for the old man in the evening of his life. We pray for all; we pray for the happy and fortunate in this world, and for the ones who suffer and do not know how to cope with their misery — that you may draw them to yourself. We pray for those who have need of conversion that you may draw them to your own way of truth; we pray for those who are already converted to you and have found life — we pray that you may draw them still closer to you. And so we pray for everyone, though we cannot name them all. Indeed, who could count all the different kinds of people? But we must mention one other group:

We pray for the servants of your Word, those whose mission it is to draw others to you, insofar as this is possible for a human being: We pray you to bless their work and themselves so that in their zeal to draw others, they themselves may not be drawn away from you. And we pray for all Christians in the community, so that drawn by you they may not have a miserable self-image, as though it were not in their power to act on your behalf and draw other people to you. We say, as far as is humanly possible, because, *though only you can draw people to yourself*, you can make use of everything and everyone to draw all to you.'

2

CALLED TO LOVE, EVEN AT THE COST OF ONE'S LIFE

Second meeting, 2 December 1982

Maximilian Kolbe: a biographical sketch

Raymond Kolbe was born in Zdunska-Wola, near Lodz in Poland, on 8 January 1894. At the age of eleven he entered the school of the Conventual Friars Minor in Leopoli, and at the age of sixteen he joined their novitiate, taking the name Maximilian. After religious profession, he came to the international college of his order in Rome to continue his studies at the Gregorian University.

In 1918 he was ordained a priest. One year before that he confided to several confrères his idea of founding what was to become his principal work: the **Army of the Immaculate.** Ecclesiastical approval was granted in 1922, after Maximilian had returned to Poland. There he founded the monthly publication *Rycerza Niepokalanej* (*'Knight of the Immaculate'*) which by 1933 enjoyed a circulation of over 1,000,000 copies.

In 1927 he founded the Niepokalanow (City of the Immaculate) a centre of religious life, promoting various forms of apostolate. In 1930 he was sent to Japan where he founded another City of the Immaculate, Mugenzai No Sono. On his return to Poland he dedicated all his energies to the Marian apostolate.

On 19 September 1939, along with some of his confreres, he was arrested by the Gestapo and deported to Germany, first to Lambsdorf and then to Amtitz concentration camp. After about three months he was allowed to return to Niepokalanow, where he resumed his religious activity. Arrested again in 1941 with four confrères, he was imprisoned at Pawiak, where he was detained longer than the others because he fell ill with pneumonia.

On 28 May he was deported to the notorious concentration camp at Auschwitz and, along with some other priests, was put into block number 17 and assigned to forced labour.

After a short time he was so exhausted and feverish that he had to be transferred to the block for those incapable of work, and finally again to block 14, where the work was somewhat lighter. On a fine evening in July one of the prisoners succeeded in escaping from this jail-block. When the fugitive could not be found, ten other prisoners were marked out to be executed, according to the regulations in force. One of them, a certain Francis Gajowniczek, kept murmuring desperately the names of his wife and children. Maximilian Kolbe stood out from the line and said to the commanding officer, 'I am a Polish Catholic priest. I would like to take the place of this man because he has a wife and children.' The substitution was accepted and Father Maximilian was put along with the other nine prisoners into the 'execution bunker' to be starved to death.

On 14 August 1941, the vigil of the Assumption, a nurse entered the bunker with an injection of poison to finish off the four prisoners who were still alive. Fr Kolbe was the last of the ten to die. According to the witness of a prisoner who returned home alive from Auschwitz, he stretched out his arm spontaneously to receive the injection, his face serene and smiling. His body was cremated along with those of all the other dead.

From the writings of Maximilian Kolbe
'The Immaculate: She is our ideal!

To come near to her, to become like her, to allow her to take possession of our hearts and of all our being that she might live and work in us and through us, that she herself may love God with our heart,... that we might belong to her without any restriction... that is our ideal.

To become actively involved in what surrounds us, to draw other souls to her so that the hearts of our neighbours may warm to her, thus extending her rule to the hearts of all people, whatever corner of the earth they live in, regardless of all differences of race, nationality and language — and not just for the present day, but also in the hearts of all who will live in every moment of historical time to the end of the world: that is our ideal. God can do everything, and he gives himself gladly to the heart dedicated to him. Between God and the soul there is a tide of love that flows back and forth. What an indescribable joy, what a great grace it is to be able to achieve one's ideal through the spending of one's life.

What better thing can I wish for you? ... I know of nothing more sublime than this word of Jesus: ''Greater love has no one than this; that a man lay down his life for his friends''.'

Biblical texts

John 15: 12-17
'This is my commandment, that you love one another as I have loved you. Greater love has no man than this, that a man lay down his life for his friends. You are my friends, if you do what I command you. No longer do I call you servants, for the servant does not know what his master is doing; but I have called you friends, for all that I have heard from my Father I have made known to you. You did not choose me, but I chose you and appointed you that you should go and bear fruit, and that your fruit should abide; so that whatever you ask the Father in my name, he may give it to you. This I command you, to love one another.'

1 John 3: 16-18
'By this we know love, that he laid down his life for us; and we ought to lay down our lives for the brethren. But if any one has this world's goods and sees his brother in need, yet closes his heart against him, how does God's love abide in him? Little children, let us not love in word or speech but in deed and in truth.'

Homily
The first model of vocation that I put to you as a message that can challenge each one of us, is Maximilian Kolbe. Without any

doubt, his life was a real success, truly fulfilled. Admittedly it was not so according to any worldly criterion of fulfilment or success, since Fr Kolbe's life ended by execution in prison. But who can doubt that his life was a genuine and total response to a calling? He lived and died in a way which we must admire as exemplary and perfect, even if perhaps not readily imitable.

The key to interpreting the spirit of Fr Maximilian is this expression of Jesus, 'A man can have no greater love than to lay down his life for his friends' *(Jn 15:13)*, and the parallel text from the first letter of the same John, where he repeats the Lord's words about love.

I chose these two texts because in recent times two popes, our chief interpreters of the history of the Church and of the lives of the saints, have used them both to illustrate the life of Fr Kolbe. At his beatification ceremony, Paul VI declared: 'Within this immense ante-chamber of death, behold there was a powerful Word of life — the statement of Jesus which reveals the mystery of innocent suffering: "There is no greater love than to give one's life for one's friends."' And on 10 October 1982, at the canonisation of Fr Kolbe by John Paul II, the Pope began his sermon with: 'No one has greater love than this, to give his life for his friends! Today the Church desires to honour as a saint this man to whom it was granted to fulfil these words of our Redeemer in all their literal force.'

Both pontiffs therefore have invited us to seek the meaning of this martyrdom in the two texts which we have heard.

I would like to help share this meaning with you. First we shall briefly re-read the Scripture texts in order to bring out their essential meaning. Then we shall meditate on them, to see what these words might say to our own lives. We will end with silent Eucharist prayer, adoring Christ in the Eucharist and asking him: 'What are you requiring from me Lord? To what are you drawing me? In what direction are you prompting me in the light of these words?'

Re-reading the biblical texts

These words of the Gospel are taken from the farewell address of Jesus, which brings into focus the deep meaning of his whole

19

life. It is the moment when he reveals himself to his friends in an atmosphere full of confidence and intimacy. He speaks as we would like always to be able to speak with each other, that is, without any fear of being misunderstood, with the certainty that the listener is alert to the true and best meaning of what we are saying, and feeling secure that our partner loves us and genuinely understands what we want to communicate. So Jesus is not striving for any elegant style, fully worked out and logical. Rather, he expresses himself in language that is full of feeling; sometimes he repeats himself as we do when we are sure that every word is being understood and that even repeating ourselves is accepted as a sign of affection.

In the brief section we have taken from this long discourse, Jesus highlights four realities and relates them to each other. *The theme of the commandment*: 'This is my commandment; *the theme of love*: 'That you love one another as I have loved you, no one has greater love, I command you to love each other; *the theme of friendship*: 'To give his life for his friends; you will be my friends; I do not call you servants any longer but friends'; *the theme of choice*: 'You have not chosen me but I have chosen you.'

These four themes, *command, love, friendship, choice,* are seen by the repetition of the words in their mutual relationship and above all as they relate to Jesus. And they take on a force and a depth of meaning that are altogether *new* because they are about the person of the Lord and the gift that he is making of himself.

In the light of this fundamental reference point — Christ, who gives himself without reservation for man, the central theme of the Eucharist: *Christus traditus*, sent by the Father to us and handing himself over to death on our behalf — we can feel a new resonance and a new richness of meaning in these four common terms of command, love, friendship and choice.

Command no longer appears as something purely formal or external which comes to me from outside; rather it is something that moves me from within.

Love is no longer a generic and ambiguous reality; it becomes a personal experience at the deepest level that touches the mystery of my person.

Friendship has no pretence in it; it is genuine, perfect friendship on which we can count in an absolute and unconditional way.

The *choice* is above all from God's side; it is not we who choose but we who are chosen by God; we are called by him and by virtue of this choice we are able to choose: to choose love, friendship, life and the gift of life.

These words all come together in Jesus, who gives his life for us, and who calls us to give our own life.

In chapter three of his first letter, St John lists some conditions if one is to live as a child of God: to break away from sin, to observe the commandments (especially love) and to turn away from false prophets and from the dominant culture.

The text we have read illustrates the second of these conditions: to keep the commandments, above all love. The fundamental message is about love and includes two aspects. In the first the emphasis is upon love and its opposites: 'This is the message you have heard, that you should love one another'; and some things that oppose love are mentioned: 'Not like Cain who came from the evil one and killed his brother... do not be surprised if the world hates you... he who does not love remains in death... he who hates his brother is a murderer.' And so love is clearly seen in the light of its opposites: to kill or to hate or to bring death to others. The text says that, in a sense, not to love is in itself to kill and this may surprise us. The text referring to the first murderer (Cain), and searching the human heart in the light of the whole of scripture invites us to see the gradual, almost inevitable but progressive and logical transition from not loving to hating and to killing. This idea might startle us and we might say that it is not true, that we are not so evil, and that not loving does not mean killing. Then let us remember the figure of Fr Kolbe; not only was he killed; but he was one of 4,000,000 people who were coldly killed because of unmotivated hatred, a satanic hatred that arose from non-loving. It is a chilling example of how non-love is connected with hatred and hatred with death. This is the first point in the text.

The second point develops the positive aspect: 'By this we know love, that he gave his life for us.' If non-love is to kill, love is to give life as Christ has shown. To make it more concrete, St John — knowing well that literally to give one's life is something that only a few people like Fr Kolbe are called upon to do — explains with practical wisdom that to give one's life means to give something of oneself, beginning with not closing one's heart to others: 'If someone has the riches of this world, material or cultural advantages, friendship, time, good health — and seeing his brother in need, closes his heart to him, how can the love of God dwell in him?'

To love is to give life, to expend one's life, to give something of oneself, not to shut one's heart.

Points for meditation

I invite you to re-read these two passages attentively during our moment of silence, in order to assimilate them, to taste the words of Jesus, the words of the apostle and the reality that stands behind them: that is that Christ gave life and the relationship between love and death.

This relationship is not easy to express because the idea of death cannot be immediately deduced in some analytic way from the word Love. Nevertheless it appears in fact and not only in a negative way, that not to love is to hate and to hate brings death, whereas to love genuinely is to love unconditionally even to death.

This truth becomes evident not only in Jesus, not only in Fr Kolbe, but at least in some way in whoever truly loves, in whoever has some living experience of that wonderful self-transcendence which is love. It is the capacity to go out from oneself and from one's own self-interest for the sake of another, even to the point of sacrificing everything, or at least having profound willingness to sacrifice much — very much — on account of love.

This text gives us a way of glimpsing the mysterious love of God for us. God is the gift of himself, the gift of life. He is the one who loves so passionately, so unconditionally, even to death itself. The love of God for man in Jesus for us is a serious love; it is authentic passion. And if God is like this for us, this gives us some insight into the mystery of God himself. As John says: 'God is love,' love understood in the unconditional, deep, total sense which we find in the text we have just read together.

Father Kolbe's response to love

In what way does Fr Kolbe enable us to see life and death as answering a call, and as a vocation to total self-giving? 'Maximilian did not simply die but he gave his life for his brother. In that terrible death there was all the greatness of a definitive act and of a human choice. Therefore he did not merely die but he gave his life. This was not a mere biological fatality; of his own will he offered himself to death out of love, and in this, is seen the definitive greatness of a human act'. *(John Paul II, 1 October 1982).*

These words of the Pope invite us to meditate on the link between love and human choice. If the perfection of the human being, his definitive choice, is love and if love is perfected when it attains to giving one's life then (we understand) in the action of Fr Kolbe there appears not only the whole heroism of a human choice, but also the greatness of every vocation understood as the choice of an action that perfectly responds to a calling.

In Maximilian's supreme action is made clear what is implicit in any full reply to God's total call. This call is involved in each baptised person's vocation, which is a call to total self-giving. Fr Kolbe lived it in a dramatic way. His life story may surprise us on account of his great love for Mary which urged him to such a fever of apostolic activity. Some might wonder whether his enthusiasm, his zeal, all this doing which occupied his life, were authentic. What put the seal upon all the particular choices of his everyday life was the way he died: This shows that behind all the actions of his life there was a choice of love that was absolute and definitive.

Questions for us

The same thing is true for each of us. We also make partial choices every day. They are authentic only if they are supported by a definitive choice, by a response to the call that God gave us in baptism and which the Holy Spirit continually develops within us. It is the vital force of the Eucharist which draws us in all our individual options and guides us towards the definitive choice of life.

Maximilian Kolbe was inspired throughout his life by the

23

Immaculate Madonna to whom he entrusted both his love for Christ and his desire for martyrdom. In the mystery of the Mother of God he could contemplate the marvellous power of the divine grace that is offered to humanity.

Reflecting on these texts of St John, which throw light both on the existence of Fr Kolbe and on every human existence, we can now ask ourselves a *first* question: What is my definitive calling, and to what am I called? In what way do I understand my own life as a call? Am I ready to orientate that life in such a way as to listen to God's call?

And a *second* question: Do I keep my heart closed to anybody? If so, then the love of God does not dwell in me and I am not responding to my life as to a call. I may appear to do so but in fact, and at a deeper level, there is something missing in my response.

If the first question is on a broader scale, the second one reaches more concretely into the quality of our everyday life. And if my heart has been closed to someone, how can I now show that person that this is not my definitive attitude, but rather that I would now like to open myself to him or to her as Jesus opened himself to me?

And now silently adoring Jesus in the Eucharist — the fullness of that attraction which reaches out to every Christian calling — let us pray for one another, so that even if we cannot imitate Fr Kolbe in the heroism of his death we may at least know a sharing in that power of love which gave him strength to respond to his ultimate calling.

3

THE DARKNESS OF FAITH

Third meeting, 6 January 1983
Biographical sketch: Thérèse of the Child Jesus
Thérèse Martin was born at Alençon (France) on 2 January, 1873, the child of Louis and Celia Martin, whose simple and generous faith had a deep influence on their daughters.

When Celia died in 1877, Louis Martin brought Thérèse and her sisters to Lisieux where, as a fifteen-year-old, she entered the convent of Carmel in 1888, taking the name of Sister Thérèse of the Child Jesus and of the Holy Face. She made her religious profession on 8 September 1890 and, after a short life in the heroic exercise of faith and love towards God and his Church, she died at the age of twenty-four on 13 September 1897.

Her doctrinal teaching, which developed during the course of her religious life and was recorded in her *Autobiographical Manuscript* is quite straightforward. It is popularly known as *the Little Way* and involves setting aside any confidence in external achievements, in favour of *the pure sentiment of love* (more effective than any justice based upon works). Thérèse goes directly to the heart of the Gospel, where the good news of divine mercy freely granted marks the decisive passage from the Old to the New Testament. The more we discover her *little way* the more we understand that it is, in fact, the *only* way. It is the way of pure faith and pure love, with the conscious acceptance of not seeing the path ahead, and of remaining weak and imperfect. As is often the case with the saints, Thérèse began at the point when the majority of Christians are ready to give up.

Extracts from the *Autobiographical Manuscript*
'At that time I enjoyed a faith so living and so clear that the

thought of Heaven formed all of my happiness and I could scarcely believe that there was anyone so foolish as to reject this belief.

I thought they were going against their real, personal beliefs when they denied the existence of Heaven, that beautiful Heaven where God himself wishes to be their eternal reward.

But in the festival days after Easter, Jesus caused me to understand that there really *are* souls without faith, people who through the abuse of God's grace have lost this great treasure, the source of the only joy that is pure and true. He allowed my soul to be invaded by the deepest darkness, so that the thought of Heaven which used to be so sweet for me now brought with it nothing but struggle and torment... This trial was destined to last not just for a few days, nor for a few weeks. It will end only at the hour appointed by the merciful God, and that hour... has not yet arrived.

I would like to be able to explain better what I feel, but alas I'm afraid that is impossible. A person must actually make the journey through this dark tunnel in order to understand its blackness. But I will try to explain it by means of a comparison. Suppose I had been born in a place normally covered by thick fog but I had once caught a glimpse of a beautiful landscape, with the whole of nature transfigured by the splendour of the sun. From my infancy I had heard others speak about this marvellous wonder, but now I know that the place where I was born is not my real homeland. But there is another far better place, where I hope one day to live. This is not just a story invented by an inhabitant of the sorry place where I live. It is rather a sure reality, because the king of that other land of glory has come to live for thirty-three years in our land of shadows. But alas, the darkness did not understand that this divine king is the Light of the World.

O Lord, your daughter has understood your divine light. She begs you to forgive her unbelieving brothers; she accepts to share the bread of sorrow for as long a time as you wish, and she does not ask to rise from this bitter table at which poor sinners eat until the time that you decide. In her own name and in the name of her brothers she simply asks, "Have mercy on us Lord, for we are poor sinners!

26

O Lord, make us holy... May all those who are not yet enlightened by the bright light of faith finally come to see it''.... Jesus, if it is necessary that the table they have spoiled should be purified by a soul that loves you, I am prepared to eat alone this bread of suffering until it pleases you to bring me into your kingdom of light. The only grace I ask of you is that I may never offend you. Ah dear mother, what I am writing is topsy turvy! ...

I said that from my infancy I was sure that one fine day I would pass from this sad and shadowy place. For not only did I believe what I heard from others wiser than myself but in the depth of my own heart I had a great longing for a more beautiful land. But then the fog grew thick around me — so dense that it penetrates my very soul and wraps it round in such a way that I can no longer find within me the sweet image of my true home. Everything has disappeared. And when I want to rest my weary heart from the darkness that surrounds it, by remembering the bright place of my desires, my torment only increases. The darkness seems to speak with the voice of sinners, mocking me: ''You dream of light, of your sweetly-perfumed homeland! You long to possess eternally the Creator of all this wonderful world. You hope to escape one day from the fog that surrounds you. Go on, go on! You'll see what death will bring you — not what you hope for but only a darker night: the night of nothingness!''

My dear mother, the picture I have tried to give of the darkness that surrounds my soul is so sketchy and imperfect; but I don't dare to write any more about it for fear of blaspheming... I'm afraid I've already said too much...

May Jesus forgive me if I have displeased him. But he knows very well that even without feeling the joy of the faith I try my best to carry out its duties. I believe I have made more acts of faith in the last year that in all of my previous life.'

Biblical text

Mark 14: 32-38
'They went to a place which was called Gethsemane; and he said to his disciples, ''Sit here, while I pray.'' And he took with him

Peter and James and John, and began to be greatly distressed and troubled. And he said to them, "My soul is sorrowful, even to death; remain here, and watch." And going a little farther, he fell on the ground and prayed that, if it were possible, the hour might pass from him. And he said, "Abba, Father, all things are possible to thee; remove this cup from me; yet not what I will, but what thou wilt." And he came and found them sleeping, and he said to Peter, "Simon, are you asleep? Could you not watch one hour? Watch and pray that you may not enter into temptation; the spirit is willing, but the flesh is weak".'

Homily

From this gospel text of St Mark, let me draw attention to three words that describe the state of the soul endured by Jesus on that night of agony in the Garden of Olives. He began to feel *fear* and *anguish*, and he said to them, 'My soul is *sad* even to death.' It is clear that Jesus had the experience of *sadness*, *fear* and *anguish*. We must ask ourselves what place these realities have in a person's life and in what sense are they part of our response to a calling.

The experience of inner wounding

The experience of Thérèse of Lisieux can help us understand this part of the gospel. The passage we have read from her writings contains some significant parallels to what is said about Jesus in Gethsemane. For example, where she speaks of the 'fog that surrounds me and penetrates my soul', of a 'torment which increases', or where she says, 'I don't want to write any more for fear of blaspheming'. And again, when she speaks of 'deeper darkness', of 'struggle and torment', and of this lasting 'not just for a few days or a few weeks.'

In order that the Lord may give us an understanding of this experience, let me draw your attention to a text from Paul's letter to the Romans, where the Apostle uses a similar kind of vocabulary: 'I am speaking the truth, I am not lying... I have great sorrow and unceasing anguish in my heart' *(9: 1-2)*. St Paul then takes up the words of Jesus, which we have seen as

28

belonging to the experience of Thérèse — real sorrow, deep anguish. He then goes on: 'I could wish that I were accursed and cut off from Christ for the sake of my brethren, my kinsmen by race.' Accursed and separated from Christ! These terms have something of the flavour, almost of the blasphemy about which the Carmelite saint wrote in her diary. I feel that we are talking about two similar experiences which could be described as a laceration of the spirit, *an inner wounding*, or violent division within the person. This deep inner split arises from a traumatic state of mind, a terrible tension.

What is the cause of this tension? The apostle expresses it perhaps more clearly: on the one side Paul belongs to Christ, his whole love is for Christ, for God, and he lives an absolute, unconditional loyalty to the mystery of Christ; on the other side he feels a strong bond with his own people and race, his Jewish family; and grieving at their incredulity towards the Gospel, he still feels associated with it as though it were his own unbelief. And from this comes his deep inner tension or wound, which is expressed in the phrase, 'Great sorrow and unceasing anguish.'

It is the suffering of a person who, without any question, feels united to God, and yet at the same time feels solidarity with humanity, with his brethren, with others whose destiny, hopes and anxieties he completely shares. Paul lives the extreme difficulty and, in the end, the incompatibility of this twofold and unshakable solidarity which he carries as an unresolved conflict within himself.

It is the same laceration lived by Thérèse who was drawn so strongly towards the luminous homeland and yet was totally surrounded by a dark, bleak landscape of impenetrable fog. She also uses the other image of being seated at a table full of bitter foods which she shared with unbelieving sinners. She was convinced of belonging totally and irresistibly to God and on the other hand of sharing the situation of the non-believer: 'To share with them to the point of blasphemy.' Those bleak words of Thérèse allude to a most deep inner laceration (not for a few days or a few weeks) which she was still going through as she wrote and which she would experience up to the point of her death.

Solidarity with God and with others

This is an experience of darkness of the twofold loyalty, of being unable to escape from that tension which penetrates and wounds her: 'The description I have given is such an imperfect account of the reality'; 'I would like to express what I feel but I'm afraid it's impossible: You have to pass through this dark tunnel to understand its blackness.'

It is being wounded through solidarity with people, especially those who suffer most, who are most abandoned, who feel the absurdity and senselessness of life; and yet, it is unswerving, absolute *loyalty* to God, his providence, his truth and holiness — these were the two truths lived by Thérèse of Lisieux.

So she shared that inner wounding which Jesus himself felt, and of which St Mark's Gospel (*chapter 14*) speaks. I have tried to explain it in my pastoral letter *I will draw all to myself*, when I wrote: 'Instead of letting himself be drawn into this spiral of hatred and violence, Jesus preferred to go to death on the cross, letting himself be drawn by the love of the Father with whom he is one in the very depth of his being. He obeys, loves, forgives, prays, hopes, even while grieved to his very depths by this mortal tension; that is, he shared fully in the love of God for man and yet was in solidarity with man who is a sinner separated from God' (*p. 68*)

It is the mystery of Jesus in the garden, the suffering of the Son of God, in which Thérèse shares in a mystical way, though it seems outside our experience and perhaps scarcely comprehensible. It is the mystery of Jesus upon the cross who abandons himself fully to the Father and yet shares the faith of sinful humanity so as to spare himself nothing of the grief of human experience.

The redemptive power of suffering

Yet strangely — and we see it in the final page from Thérèse of Lisieux which we have just read — this suffering can somehow attract. It has a fascinating and redemptive power: to let oneself be seriously committed for God and for humankind without denying either the one or the other.

Every genuine Christian vocation includes some call to enter, even if in a less dramatic and costly way, into that darkness felt by Jesus himself, in Gethsemane and on the cross, into the experience of Thérèse of Lisieux; to enter into a complete involvement with God — in his mysterious reality and hidden plans — without thereby abandoning contact with actual, real people in all their suffering, isolation and troubles.

There is no vocation without this tension accepted and lived as a sharing of the suffering of Jesus. There is no married vocation without the willingness to assume as one's own the sufferings of the partner; that is to go out from oneself, from one's own ego, to let oneself be caught up in absolute loyalty to the plan of God and loyalty to the person to whom we promise ourselves.

There is no religious or priestly vocation unless one is willing to go out from oneself, from one's own ivory tower, so that one is grasped by total fidelity to the mystery of God and the mystery of humanity.

And if it sometimes appears to us that the lives of particular people appear, externally, to be wasted existences, it is perhaps because they have not entered into this kind of involvement. They are closed in themselves, they have not accepted the challenge of this inner laceration and therefore they do not reach either God or others.

Thérèse shows us a vocation which succeeded perfectly because she did accept this inner wounding and lived it with the certainty that she would be healed in Jesus dying on the cross.

The soul of every vocation is, therefore, allowing oneself to be fully involved in the dynamic which includes, on the one side God in his absoluteness, and on the other side, with history and all that it demands of us.

Questions for ourselves
The Gospel text that we have related to Thérèse's life and experience raises some important questions:

(a) Do I accept, and to what extent do I allow myself to become involved? Why am I afraid to enter into this involving and transforming experience which God himself offers to me?

(b) What concrete acts of sharing could I undertake from now on in the family, in my study or work situation, in my relations with others?

Often a family comes into crisis because of an insufficient experience of involvement: All of us doing our own thing, living in our own world and not caring about the others, much less about the plan of God. The same can be true of the school, the work-place, the parish, the group. What concrete thing could I do immediately to show that I also wish to get involved in the fullness of my calling?

4

TO MAKE RELIGION INTO LOVE

Fourth meeting, 2 February 1983

Biographical sketch: Charles de Foucauld

Charles de Foucauld was born in Strasbourg on 15 September 1858. He lived a thoughtless and sceptical adolescence. At the age of seventeen he decided to opt for a military career and chose the Academy of St Cyr because the examination there was easier than others. But Charles got on badly there and ended by being expelled for laziness and occasional terrible fits of anger.

He went to the cavalry school at Saumur. If at St Cyr he was punished for laziness, here the problem was that he was undisciplined. Among his colleagues he became famous as an organiser of parties: his primary ambition was to enjoy life as much as possible.

In 1881 his regiment went to Africa to see action in South Oran. Eager to be involved in this campaign at any price Charles sought to be allowed back into the army (even as a simple soldier rather than with the rank of lieutenant which he had held earlier). He threw himself into soldiering as he had thrown himself into enjoyment — as a way of escaping from the sadness that he felt deep down in himself. During his short time as a soldier he showed great bravery, prepared for any kind of risk or sacrifice.

In 1882 he left the army to become an explorer, going first to Algiers for a period of study and research. By this time he wanted to prove his worth: his journey into the interior of Morocco in 1883 was the first exploration of that area by a European. During this journey of exploration he was deeply touched by the unceasing invocation of God all around him. The summons to prayer, the men who prostrated themselves five times a day towards the east, the constant invocation of the name of Allah in conversation and in writing, the whole range of Muslim devotion of life caused him to ask himself: 'Why am I such an un-religious man?' The seed of dissatisfaction was sown in his heart.

One evening, quite by chance, Charles met Fr Hugelin who had been friendly for some time with the de Foucauld family. That meeting marked the beginning of his conversion. Increasingly from then on, like a rising tide, his life was characterised by one unquenchable desire: the imitation of Christ.

Charles himself notes three fundamental dates in his journey: 1886 (his conversion), 1890 (his joining the Trappists), 1897 (his leaving the Trappists and beginning his individual journey).

In December 1916 at Tammanrasset in the Sahara Desert, as he was coming out from adoring the Blessed Sacrament, Charles de Foucauld was murdered by a young Tuareg.

From the writings of Charles de Foucauld
While I was in Paris for the printing of my book about the journey in Morocco...I met with some virtuous Christian people who were very intelligent and I said to myself — pardon the expression but it is exactly what I thought at the time — that perhaps this religion was not absurd after all.

At the same time a very strong inner grace was spurring me on. I began to go to Church and I was happiest when I was there and passed long hours repeating this strange prayer: 'My God, if you exist, help me to know you.'

I became convinced that I ought to be better informed about this religion in which perhaps I might find that truth which I was desperately seeking and I thought that the best thing would be to take some instruction in the Catholic religion. Someone told me about a very educated priest who had been a student at the École Normale. I found him in his confessional but I said that I had not come for confession because I was not a proper believer but I wanted more information about the Catholic faith.

The good God who had so effectively begun the work of my conversion through that strong inner grace which urged me almost irresistibly forward also brought it to completion. The priest, previously unknown to me, to whom God had sent me, and who combined culture with real virtue and even greater goodness, became my confessor and has been my best friend over the past fifteen years....

No sooner had I come to believe that God existed than I understood that there was nothing else for me to do but live for him alone: My religious vocation was born at the same moment as my faith: God is so great. There is such a difference between God and all that is not him.

(From a letter to Henry de Castliese)

With all my strength I wanted to demonstrate to these poor lost brothers that our religion is all love and brotherhood, that its symbol is the heart; to hold conversation with them, to give them medicines, alms and hospitality in my camp, to be a brother to them, to tell them that we are all brothers in God and that we all hope to arrive one day in the same paradise; to pray for the Tuareg with all my heart: that is my life.

(From the letters, no. 51)

Prayer

My father, I abandon myself to you,
make of me what you want,
whatever you make of me I thank you.
I am ready for everything, I accept everything
as long as your will is done in me and in all creatures.
I desire nothing else, my God.
Into your hands I commend my Spirit.
I give it over, O God, with all the love of my heart,
because I love you, and for me it is a necessity of love to give myself and hand myself over to you without measure, with infinite trust, for you are my Father.

Biblical text

Acts 22: 3-21
'I am a Jew, born at Tarsus in Cilicia, but brought up in this city at the feet of Gamaliel, educated according to the strict manner of the law of our fathers, being zealous for God as you

are all this day. I persecuted this Way to the death, binding and delivering to prison both men and women, as the High Priest and the whole council of elders bear me witness. From them I received letters to the brethren, and I journeyed to Damascus to take those also who were there and bring them in bonds to Jerusalem to be punished.

As I made my journey I drew near to Damascus, about noon a great light from heaven suddenly shone about me. And I fell to the ground and heard a voice saying to me: "Saul, Saul, why do you persecute me?" and I answered, "Who are you, Lord?" and he said to me, "I am Jesus of Nazareth whom you are persecuting." Now those who were with me saw the light but did not hear the voice of the one who was speaking to me and I said, "What shall I do Lord?" and the Lord said to me, "Rise, and go into Damascus, and there you will be told all that is appointed for you to do." And when I could not see because of the brightness of that light I was led by the hand by those who were with me and came into Damascus. And one Ananias, a devout man, according to the law, well-spoken of by all the Jews who lived there, came to me, and standing by me said to me, "Brother Saul, receive your sight". And at that very hour I received my sight and saw him and he said, "The God of our fathers appointed you to know his will to see the just one and to hear a voice from his mouth for you will be a witness for him to all men of what you have seen and heard. And now why do you wait? Rise and be baptised and wash away all your sins calling on his name." When I had returned to Jerusalem and was praying in the temple I fell into a trance and saw him saying to me, "Make haste and get quickly out of Jerusalem because they will not accept your testimony about me." And I said, "Lord, they themselves know that in every synagogue I imprisoned and beat those who believed in thee. And when the blood of Stephen thy witness was shed, I also was standing by and approving and keeping the garments of those who killed him." And he said to me, "Depart, for I will send you far away to the Gentiles.'"

Homily

For this evening's meeting we take our main thought from Charles de Foucauld while keeping also in mind the Roman pilgrimage which so many people of Milan are making these days along with the Archbishop. Rome indeed was a very important goal for Charles de Foucauld.

First of all, because after being in various parts of the world and having struggled a long time searching for the way he should go, it was in Rome that Charles reached a clear understanding of his vocation when the Father General of the Trappists suggested to him what might be God's will. From that moment he left behind the traditional monastic structures and began a personal journey which led him into the Sahara Desert. In Rome, therefore, his vocation became 'mission' and his very personal choice became a great act of obedience.

Secondly, because in Rome he was strengthened in a desire that was already born in him in Syria, in response to a tragic religious situation in which the Armenians were being persecuted and many of them killed. At that time he began to think about martyrdom and even to desire it as the highest way of witnessing his personal faith in Jesus Christ and the Gospel. While in Rome he often went to the Basilica of St Paul outside the walls or he stopped to look at the Colosseum, meditating on the courageous witness given by those first martyrs of Christianity who deeply impressed him. Gradually he discovered that God was calling him to the daily sacrifice of his life for the sake of the Gospel; in the end this made him worthy literally to give his life for the Lord's name. His death came violently at Tammanrasset in 1916.

So this evening we can feel ourselves united with Rome, with the Roman martyrs, with the Pope in Rome, with our Archbishop who has just become a Cardinal there, and who, officially, in the presence of his people undertakes solemnly to witness to the Gospel even unto death. Let us enter into a deep bond with the Church and all of our brothers who live and die for the Lord.

How he found God

What is the pathway along which Charles de Foucauld found God? He himself answers this question in two of his writings. One of them we have just read, the letter to his friend Henry de Castriese who was going through a crisis of faith. Charles seeks to illuminate his friend's problem by telling him what happened to himself when he found the Lord.

In another of his writings he tells of his experience during a spiritual retreat. This takes the form of a prayer, giving praise to the divine mercy that brought him from afar where he had hidden, to lead him to the fullness of light.

The pathway he followed was above all *restlessness of the heart.* He says of himself that, at the age of seventeen, something was dead within him; that, in the middle of the extravagant parties that he organised with such great energy, the saddest member in the whole company was himself. His adolescence and youth were afflicted by that inner sadness which did not allow him ever to be at peace or satisfied. There is a kind of sadness which is a grace that one experiences when one is distanced from God. It is one of the ways in which God strongly reveals himself by letting us feel his absence as a cause of unhappiness.

There is a second element which enters in a determining way in Charles de Foucauld's path of discovery towards God: It was his meeting with some people and one in particular, a cousin of his named Mary, who was like a mother to him (his own mother had died when he was only a child). This woman did not speak much about religion and especially she did not try to persuade him during those years when he was living in a state of religious indifference or of outright atheism. She was a Christian and she showed it in the humility and the simplicity of her daily life.

She influenced him through her example only and she followed that advice which was so dear to Fr Hugelin, her spiritual director, who would become the future spiritual guide of Charles de Foucauld himself: 'If you want to convert somebody, do not try to convince him by argument. The best system is not to preach but to let him know that you love him.'

At a certain point in the life of de Foucauld something

happened which can hardly be explained in the category of psychology or sociology. This young man who called himself an atheist began to come into churches to pray and sit alone in some dark corner or behind a pillar and pray to God in this way: 'Lord, if you exist, let me come to know you.'

Although we may say that whoever searches for God will find him, it is even more true to say that God is found by the ones he himself has sought and found and captured and converted to himself.

The story of the conversion of Paul that we have heard from the Acts of the Apostles throws light on this. On the road to Damascus he was a persecutor but at the end of his journey he is an apostle. Charles de Foucauld expresses this sense of being invaded by the power of the Lord while praying to a God whom he has not yet met.

But we should add that in Charles' case the meeting with God happened also *because he sought and found a spiritual guide.* He sought an intelligent priest, well-educated in theology but one even more profound in his spiritual insight. To the young man who said to him: 'I have come for instruction about the Catholic religion since I have not really got the faith.' The priest replied 'Listen, kneel down' and heard his confession. Then he gave him the Eucharist. Fr Hugelin's action was not as brusque as it might seem. He saw what perhaps many others might not have recognised, that Charles did not need a lot of reasoning about the faith because he had already done so much of it himself. What he needed rather was a word that would encourage him to take the step that he was ready to take. And at that point the young man suddenly discovered God and decided to live for him *alone.*

Perhaps all of us who are gathered here believe that we have encountered God. But I would like to invite you to read again the story of Paul on the road to Damascus and the story of Charles de Foucauld to understand what it means to really encounter God and what are the pathways along which one must usually walk in order that the discovery may take place.

To help others encounter God
In which way did Charles de Foucauld choose to help others

encounter God? It was friendship. We can come back on some other phrases on that letter we have read *(n.51)* that show a great wisdom and depth.

'With all my strength I desire to show to these poor lost brothers that our religion is all love and brotherhood, that its symbol is the heart. To hold conversations with them and give them medicines, alms, hospitality in my camp, to show myself their brother, to repeat that we are all brothers in God, that we all hope to arrive one day in the same paradise, to pray for the Tuareg with all my heart, that is my life.

Above all, to prepare the ground in silence through goodness, contact, good example; having established contact, to let myself be known by them and come to know them; to love them deeply from the heart, to let them esteem and love me; in this way to break down prejudices and win their trust, gain standing with them — and this requires time. Then I must speak privately with the best disposed among them, going forward carefully in a different way with each one in such a way as to give to each what he is capable of receiving…. If they meet with Christians who are wiser or more virtuous than themselves they may then be willing to admit that perhaps these men are not in error, and be ready to ask God for enlightenment.'

Underlying this letter is surely his own personal experience of discovering God through the friendly presence of his cousin Mary. We should add that in the life of Charles de Foucauld the apostolate of friendship is much more than just a method, it is his very vocation which he would summarise in one word: Nazareth. 'The mystery which God calls me to live is that of the hidden life of Jesus in Nazareth'. After much searching he was drawn to realise this mystery fully in the Sahara among the Tuareg.

Nazareth represents the mystery of a hiddenness which is achieved not by separating oneself from others but by immersing oneself evermore in the lives of others. So Charles went in search of those who were most impoverished and, living among them, disappeared from society. He became a Tuareg among the Tuareg, crossing the desert with them on camelback, sharing in their daily life, studying their language, becoming expert in it and leaving behind all other possible ways of life (and many were open to him) in order to devote all his affection and all his abilities to these people.

His primary aim, and one that we can take as a fundamental characteristic of the apostolate and of sharing the faith, was to show the faith in practice through presence, through a style of life, through nearness, understanding others, listening to them, carrying their burdens, sharing in their real questions and desires, trying to become a model of hope and light for others. There is no kind of Christian vocation that can ignore this aspect of practical witness: actions must come before words; before verbal proclamation must come sharing a generous and loving presence to others, showing that love that Jesus in the Gospel lays down as the distinctive sign of his disciples.

If we imitate the spirit of Charles de Foucauld in living our own vocation, others who meet us will be helped to find God and — however humbly, silently or simply we do it — we can be the Lord's instrument through whom he *draws people to himself.*

Eucharist and vocation
In a little while, we will go on to silent meditation before the blessed Sacrament. From the time of his visit to Nazareth right up to the end of his life, Charles de Foucauld devoted many hours to Eucharistic adoration. So also do the two congregations, the Little Brothers of Jesus and the Little Sisters of Jesus; their Rule follows Charles in requiring them to spend at least one hour each day in adoration,which is not to be omitted under any circumstance.

From my own experience I can tell you of young people who made important decisions about their future, sometimes involving radical changes in their lifestyle, resulting from prolonged adoration of the Eucharist.

So let us pray to the Lord on each other's behalf, to stir up in us a more vital desire to worship him, to understand that the forthcoming Eucharistic Congress can transform our communities, our families and our personal lives, if it is centred on genuine adoration of the Lord.

One final point about Charles de Foucauld that I would like

to share with you: When he was converted and thought of becoming a monk, reckoning that as the highest form of self-sacrifice, his spiritual director gave him this letter of introduction to the Abbot of Solèmnes: 'Most Reverend Father, the bearer of this letter, Charles de Foucauld, is an ex-army officer, a daring explorer in Morocco, a fervent pilgrim to the Holy Land, a true gentleman and a genuine Christian, who *makes religion a matter of love.* For some time now, I have noted how his tastes and desires are leading him towards monastic life. For many months, he has felt the need of, and has been living by, its ideals. My advice is that he test his vocation for a while in Solèmnes, and I would be grateful if you, Reverend Father, would give him that opportunity to see and to live monastic life among you. I have known de Foucauld for years. He is absolutely trustworthy and I believe his vocation is genuine — if not for Solèmnes, then for some other monastic community. I would think of Solèmnes'.

The phrase to stress and which sums up Charles de Foucauld's whole existence from his conversion is *to make religion a matter of love.* It is what I wish for each one of you.

5

WAITING ON GOD

Fifth meeting, 3 March 1983

Biographical sketch: Simone Weil

Simone Weil was born of a Jewish family in Paris in 1909. She attended the École Normale at a precociously early age, and followed a course of philosophical studies.

After graduation, she taught philosophy with great enthusiasm for several years, while at the same time feeling a personal need to come to grips more deeply and directly with ordinary life, with its problems and sorrows. So began her committed search for truth, which she pursued with great courage in a sort of purifying suffering. She sought leave of absence from teaching and went to work at the furnaces of the Renault factory. Her unstable health was unequal to the task; she became ill and had to abandon factory work.

She was attracted to Christianity but she never came around to asking for the Sacraments despite a real desire to do so.

For a short time she lived in Marseilles. Then, being a Jewess, she had to hide and managed to escape to America. But a temperament like hers was not content to live for long in a safe and too peaceful place. She returned to Europe and in 1942 settled in London, where she continued her inner struggle and suffering. But this was not enough; she made an unsuccessful attempt to join the French Resistance and had to remain on in England. The lifestyle she practised was too much for her strength. She was brought to hospital suffering from hunger and tuberculosis and died there in 1942, at the age of only thirty-three.

The quality of her character has been well described by Charles Bo: 'In all the phases of her short human life we see the desire to restore balance to an age threatened by evil, through the offering and even the sacrifice of her own personality. This aim will help us understand the motive for some of her behaviour. It will also explain why she strongly rejected any kind of political exploitation of her actions. Simone Weil was always on the side of the oppressed, of any group threatened by defeat through force and violence. So we can understand why she joined the Spanish Communists and later her desire to go in person to Russia when it was invaded by the Germans. She has one thing to teach us, which we too often forget; it is this: whoever wants a genuine spiritual sharing with others must base it on their real life, on their sufferings and endurance. This indeed is the Catholic idea of love, that love which saves faith itself.'

From the writings of Simone Weil

'From the infinity of space and time the infinitely more infinite love of God comes to court us. He comes at his own time. We can only choose to accept and welcome him or to reject him. If we are deaf to him, he keeps coming back like a beggar but one day, also like a beggar, he will return no more.

If we are willing, God plants a little seed in us and goes away. From that moment, God has nothing more to do — nor we either, except to wait. We must only never regret saying Yes to him, our nuptial Yes. This is not so simple as it sounds, because the growth of the seed within us is painful. Indeed in order to allow it to grow, we cannot but destroy whatever puts obstacles in its way; that is, pluck up the undergrowth and the weeds. Unfortunately the weeds are deep-rooted in our own flesh and so the gardening to be done has to be violent. Still the seed, independent of the gardening, does grow by itself. One day the time will come when the soul belongs to God; that day the soul will not only agree to love but will love in truth, effectively. Then in its turn it must cross the universe to go to God.' (From *Waiting on God*)

'There is an effort to be made which is by far the most difficult of all, but it does not enter into the realm of action. It is keeping our gaze fixed on God, turning back to him when we have been distracted, devoting ourselves to him with all the intensity of

44

which we are capable. This is very hard, because the whole mediocre part of us — which is ourselves, that which we call our ego — feels condemned to death by this turning of the gaze towards God. And our ego does not want to die. It makes up all possible lies for turning away from him.

One great lie arises from pleasure or pain. We know all too well the omissions or the actions which arise from the attraction of pleasure or the fear of pain, and which force us to take our gaze away from God. When we let this happen, we imagine that we have been overcome by pleasure or pain; but often that is merely an illusion. Frequently, pleasure and pain are just the pretexts used by our mediocre ego to separate our attention from God. In themselves, neither pleasure nor pain is all that powerful. It is not so difficult to renounce a pleasure however attractive, or to submit to a pain even if severe; many ordinary people do it every day. But it is infinitely difficult to set aside even the lightest pleasure or expose oneself to the most simple pain purely for God — for the true God, for him who is in the heavens and nowhere else — because when you do this you are heading not towards suffering but towards annihilation, a death more radical than the death of the flesh and one that nature abhors. It is the death of that which we call ego.' (From *Disordered thoughts upon the love of God*)

Biblical text

Mark 7: 24-30
'And from there he arose and went away to the region of Tyre and Sidon. And he entered a house, and would not have any one know it; yet he could not be hid. But immediately a woman, whose little daughter was possessed by an unclean spirit, heard of him, and came and fell down at his feet. Now the woman was a Greek, a Syro-Phoenician by birth. And she begged him to cast the demon out of her daughter. And he said to her, "Let the children first be fed, for it is not right to take the children's bread and throw it to the dogs." But she answered him, "Yes, Lord; yet even the dogs under the table eat the children's crumbs." And he said to her, "For this saying you may go your

way; the demon has left your daughter.'' And she went home,
and found the child lying in bed, and the demon gone.'

Homily

The woman whose vocation has introduced us this evening to
the reading from St Mark's Gospel was a very unusual person,
almost eccentric. More than one of you perhaps will wonder why
I speak to Christians about her. Simone Weil was a Jewess who
never made the decision to receive Baptism. What is more, her
life story was definitely marked by extremism, even belligerence.
During the Second World War she was extremely eager — but
was not allowed — to be dropped by parachute behind the
German lines and join the French Resistance, thereby risking
certain death. Later, as she lay ill with tuberculosis, the final
days of her life were almost a death through starvation: she
refused to eat because she was so keenly aware of the hunger
being endured by many of her compatriots back in France.

She was a person, therefore, who lived suffering in an almost
agonising way: her own, and especially that of others which she
made her own. Also, throughout her numerous writings, we do
not find a single ordered or balanced thought. They are full of
fragmentary notes sometimes incomplete, often paradoxical. Her
early death did not allow her to give systematic form to that
volcano of ideas, of feelings and of different gestures which
constituted her whole life.

Why then should we want to reflect upon her as a preparation
for contemplating the Gospel scene about the woman who
insistently asked Jesus to cure her daughter? Even more, one
might ask: how could Simone Weil help us on our spiritual
journey which has as its title 'Word — Eucharist — Vocation'?
How can this young Jewish woman help us here?

I would like to underline some of the qualities of Simone Weil,
which may allow us to see more clearly how a life like hers can
inspire our own vocational search. I believe she can also clarify
our reading of St Mark's story, which we may call the 'Tireless
Woman' or 'The Unceasing Search for the Good'.

46

Characteristics of Simone Weil

a) First of all, Simone Weil was a Jewess. Her belonging to God's holy people, to which so many gifts have been given, did not manifest itself primarily in external actions of Jewish ritual, but rather in that fundamental virtue which Simone herself calls *attention* and which in my opinion is the modern psychological equivalent of the Hebrew biblical theme of *listening*.

In that whole eager search for truth which painfully gripped every instant of her life, one senses that she considered the good of the person not as something to be produced but rather something to be welcomed and received: a good which comes from God. What is required on the human person's part is attention, a humble openness towards God and towards all personal situations which could be an echo of the word of God.

b) This quality of constant attention to God and to his Word, to people and especially to the poor, aroused her strong sense of *life as vocation,* a life determined by someone who calls and who requires our response.

A biographer once wrote of her that 'after months of inner darkness and almost a crisis of desperation, between the ages of fourteen and fifteen she suddenly understood that there is a fullness of truth assigned for every human being, even those who have very little natural ability.' In other words she grasped the idea of a universal vocation, based not on privilege, on beauty, on one's power to impress or on one's social prestige; rather, it is a vocation for all — even for the poorest and the least esteemed. And she grasped that there are three ways by which the human person can reach this fullness: the desire for truth, the constant effort of attention, and obedience to one's personal vocation.

Obedience to one's own vocation was the mainspring of her whole life, of that constant search which did not cease, even in her last agony.

c) A third reason for devoting attention to this most unusual witness of our times is that Simone Weil felt an irresistible attraction towards the Eucharist, even though she never formally became a Christian and a Catholic. The pages she wrote about this sacrament and especially about Eucharistic adoration must

47

rank among the most tender and expressive writings on this subject in the twentieth century. Towards the end of her life she wrote: 'I feel an intense and ever-increasing desire for Communion'. But she was prevented from taking the final step by a series of prejudices, some of them historical, some sociological, which led her to keep on reflecting on a decision that she found vexing and difficult.

As I read her, therefore, I find Simone's attitude of tireless search reminiscent of that of various women in the Gospel: the grief-stricken anguish of Mary Magdalene at the tomb, as she searched for Jesus in such a state of distress that she failed to recognise him; the attitude of the Samaritan woman towards Jesus, at first sceptical and suspicious, but later so attentive and enthusiastic; or the patient search by the Blessed Virgin Mary when Jesus left her and Joseph to stay on in Jerusalem in the temple, the house of God.

The Syro-Phoenician woman

Among the many texts that could be selected in order to meditate the message of Simone Weil in the light of God's Word, I have picked St Mark's account of the Syro-Phoenician woman because, like Simone, she was outside the borders of visible orthodoxy with the chosen people. But more strongly and successfully than Simone she continued her tireless quest, which gave her an unbounded ability to enter the very heart of God.

Let us now have a look at our Gospel text and notice its more important elements, so that it can help us to reflect and raise some questions for our own lives.

Even a simple reading of the passage shows that its centre is a dialogue which begins with the indirect statement: 'The woman begged Jesus to cast out the demon from her daughter, and the woman a Greek' *(Mk 7: 26)*. The language then becomes dialogue and opens with a very hard and cutting phrase of Jesus, 'Let the children be fed first. It is not good to take the bread from the children and throw it to the dogs.' These are words, of a kind that we would never have dared to imagine might come from Jesus.

The woman's reply is dignified and humble but at the same

time confident and insistent: 'Yes Lord, but even the little dogs beneath the table eat the crumbs the children throw away.' Then the dialogue ends with the emphatic statement of Jesus, 'For this saying you may go; the demon has left your daughter.'

In its structure, therefore, it is a combative and dramatic dialogue. It reminds us of that other biblical story about Jacob's struggle with the angel, or the exchange between Mary and Jesus at the Wedding Feast of Cana, where the Lord's mother quietly insists on her request, despite what at first seems to be his refusal.

This story comes within a very interesting context in St Mark's Gospel *(chapters 6, 7, 8)*, where there are various levels of resistance to the word of Jesus. First on the part of the apostles ('Their heart was hardened', *6:52)*; then, even more so, on the part of the pharisees and scribes ('You nullify the word of God in favour of your own traditions', *7:13)*, men who empty the word of its force. And in the middle comes this woman, who implores and begs the Lord in spite of apparent refusal. She asks for the crumbs from the table, after a reply at which she might easily have taken offence. In this gospel chapter we have the image of the satisfied, those who feel no need for guidance because they know everything already; people who *pay no attention* (using the language of Simone Weil) and to whom Jesus says: 'Do you not understand, are your hearts hardened? Having eyes, do you not see? and having ears do you not hear? and do you not remember? When I broke the five loaves for the 5,000, how many baskets full of broken pieces did you take up?' *(Mk 8:17-19)*. The apostles, the wise, the intelligent, the scribes do not understand, cannot penetrate the meaning. The woman, on the contrary, symbolises the poor, those who find hope in the Gospel and in the Church; those whose hearts are opened; people who know what they want and who can value even the crumbs and ask for them with humble insistence. The woman is a symbol of the poor one who opens and discovers the heart of God.

Searching for the true face of God and of the human person
Our brief re-reading of the Gospel text tells us for our meditation that the human word is powerful.

There is something strange about the commendation of Jesus

49

at the end of this gospel text, where he says, 'For this saying you may go your way'. He does not say, 'Through my power or by my force or by my healing power', but *'by this saying of yours'*. What a formidable praise of the human word where it is the expression of real faith which penetrates the clouds and goes beyond appearances.

Jesus at first appeared hard and apparently refused, but the woman understood that behind and despite appearances there was a divine manifestation, that is, a mercy which would not refuse the word of faith. From a psychological point of view we could say that Jesus felt himself understood. More theologically we would assert: God felt himself loved, felt that someone had unconditional trust in him; the woman had passed the test of darkness and refusal and understood it as a test of love; she believed totally in love. She believed in it because she loved her daughter so completely. The whole episode takes place on behalf of the daughter: 'My daughter, my child', not for the sake of the mother. She does not ask for herself but for another human being; she stands for the person who cares for others or for the Church which cares for humanity.

In a very real way the Canaanite woman personifies the passion, the searching, the attention which every man and woman should have in looking for the true face of God, and for the face of our brothers and sisters in their difficulties and their needs.

This passion, this tireless search shines out in the life of Simone Weil. The passage of Mark which we have read in the light of a character of our own time tells us that great human enterprises (and the life of each one of us is a great enterprise — to be responsible for our own life and that of our brother Abel) demand an unceasing search of which the sign, symbol, and execution is constant adoring prayer on behalf of wounded humanity.

We can find a striking example of this searching in the long journeys of Pope John Paul II as he goes out to the hungry and oppressed peoples who are so much in his heart. The Pope lives the same experience as that woman in the Gospel and so his passion can overcome disappointment, rejection, bitterness or threat. He too is a witness for our time.

The questions for us

What message do we get from the figure of Simone Weil, of the Syro-Phoenician woman or of the present Pope in tireless search?

They tell us that there is no vocational path, no way of finding our proper place in life without this kind of search, despite all obstacles, disinclination and even despite the silence of God. To conclude, we may put three kinds of question to ourselves:

a) Am I determined in my searching? Am I searching with prayer, with perseverance even in the midst of obscurity? Do I ask advice and try to be open? Am I risking difficult and hard things in order to learn through sacrifice what is my real calling?

b) Do I get discouraged in my search? And here our question can become a prayer. Lord, you know how often we grow tired of seeking and how if we were in the place of the Syro-Phoenician woman we would have given up after the first refusal, saying that you did not understand us. Grant us instead the grace to blame ourselves for not understanding your heart, for not having the faith to penetrate the cloud, for not grasping that you want to be understood by us.

c) What action at this time could express my desire to seek you? Would it be some act of penance during this Lent season or some action of benevolence or of pardon. Or is it some courageous action for a just cause, something that we ought to defend and support?

May our Blessed Lady help us in this unceasing search from which alone we will come to know what you call us to; may she help us understand what is the value of searching for the true face of God and the face of humanity.

6

BUILDING THE CITY OF GOD IN THE CITY OF MAN

Sixth session, 5 May 1983

Biographical sketch: Giorgio La Pira

Giorgio La Pira was born in Pozzallo in the province of Ragusa (Sicily) in 1904. He taught Roman Law at the University of Florence, and in 1938 founded *Principles*, a periodical which was soon banned by the authorities because of its clear-cut opposition to Fascism. He later joined Dossetti, Lazzati and Fanfani in *Social Chronicles*, which expressed the voice of the left wing of the Christian Democrat party during the De Gasperi years. He was among the group which drew up the Constitution for the Italian Republic, and was in his later years a most popular mayor of Florence, where he promoted some memorable schemes to foster peace and friendship between peoples.

He died in Florence, after a severe illness, on 5 November 1977. In the funeral homily, Cardinal Benelli said of him: 'This man seemed always to radiate cheerfulness and confidence, with an ease which some may have misjudged as facile, but which was actually the fruit of an intimate union with God through prayer, contemplation and a deep poverty — a state of grace which was reflected in his face. He carried his own heavy burden of suffering, something that is unavoidable for anyone who is seriously committed to Christ and his truth.'

The spirit of Giorgio La Pira can be sensed in the preface he wrote for a book about another Italian Catholic, *The Social and Political Commitment of Pier Giorgio Frassati*.[1]

1. *L'impegno sociale e politico di Pier Giorgio Frassati* (Ed. Ave, Roma, 1978). Frassati was a young man from Turin who, after a short but very intense life, died from sudden poliomyelitis at the age of twenty-four. His clear and

'To understand Pier Giorgio Frassati, we have to appreciate the interior religious, theological and metaphysical depths from which sprang the political activity which characterised his social commitment.

An observer insensitive to the vital impulses and leavening that are essential to Christianity might misjudge this young man's total involvement in the things of this world and in politics in particular as a sign of lack of interior life or of little "detachment" from the world and its values.

Can one maintain that in this young activist there was a true flowering of grace and purity? Could there be holiness amid the thousand and one distractions of such a politically active life? While one readily admits that an active charity (of the kind practised by the St Vincent de Paul Society or Catholic Action) is a sign of inner Christian authenticity, can we go further and recognise the same genuine spirituality in a life spent at such a hectic pace, engaged in journalism and propaganda on behalf of the Italian People's Party *(Partito Popolare)*?

Was all that activity a grey area that would constitute a barrier to the light of grace and the fervour of intimate prayer? Might it have been anything other than an obstacle to the full flowering of God's grace and of innocence? Does a lifestyle like this not rule out that radical purity of heart, imbued with the love of God and of his eternal values, which is the very essence of holiness?

Gratia non destruit, sed perficit (grace does not destroy, but perfects). With this phrase, St Thomas Aquinas throws a bright light upon the whole texture of human affairs. It highlights the intimate and constitutive values of the human person, values of the family, of work, of economics and of technology; social values; values of politics and of culture, art and poetry; all those values which are not rejected by Christianity as though alien to its own nature; rather, they are in a sense structural elements of Christianity itself. In the long run, Christianity is none other than the living texture of these values, purified and leavened

passionate Christian witness made him a model of lay holiness for a whole generation of young Italian Catholics.

by grace in order to be definitively perfected in glory at the end of history....

There is poverty, unemployment, a shortage of houses and of social assistance; will the charity of St Vincent de Paul suffice to solve all of this? Our first response to these things, certainly, must be the helpful compassion of the Samaritan, doing what we can to relieve the immediate need. But then we must go deeper and attack the root causes. These are problems that go back for centuries, which have given rise to deep thought and endeavour, and are marked by some of the key figures in Christian history.

What then? Then surely we must get involved in facing these problems ourselves! And the instruments for this struggle, however inadequate and unfocused they may seem at times, are the political party, the committee, elections, the press, and so forth.

Dangerous instruments, too, for the life of the spirit? Yes indeed, sometimes they do not go well together. But in many situations they are the only instruments for achieving a purpose: work for the unemployed, houses for those who need them, assistance for those who are badly off.

How can you translate the ideal of fraternity, so central to the Christian faith, into social, political and economic structures if you take no interest in these structures — if you do not get involved in renewing and reforming whatever is outdated or wrong in these structures? How can you cause your Christian yeast to leaven the world — and so form a Christian civilisation and a Christian society — if you turn your back on social and political matters?

St Thomas understood very clearly that political structures are part of the architecture of the common good: to build these structures well is the highest form of activity in the human order of things.

Different architectural proposals come from all sides: liberal, socialist, marxist and Christian. There are so many problems facing those who become involved in that agonising area which is political life!

This is the background against which we can understand the

54

activity of Pier Giorgio; the political exertions of his youthful existence have to be seen in this context and they stand out from this perspective. His activities were the fruit of that 'Lift up your eyes and see', by which the Gospel of Jesus invites us to practice a love that is both sensitive and energetic.

Seen in this light all these activities are clarified: we understand why he joined the People's Party; we understand his career as a mining engineer; we understand why he got involved in so many aspects of social and political life, All were facets of one single prism. And this prism has a single ingredient: to realise his personal Christian mission in the world...

So the question we posed at the beginning does, therefore, have an answer. Is there an incurable conflict between the inner life of grace, prayer, union with God, and an exterior life spent among the often very rusty structures of politics? No indeed: we will understand this man not by starting with the conflict between outer and inner life, but rather by seeing the religious, theological and metaphysical roots from which his intense activity sprang. Here we find a purity, a supernatural clarity in the centre of his being; from it arose, and to it returned, all his vital activity.

Pier Giorgio died young, at the age of twenty-four. It pleased the Lord to call him to himself, to the life of Paradise, in company with Mary, the angels and the saints. In his short existence, which had God alone for its light, the plan he pursued was to reveal to many people the value of the mission to which life calls everyone: to bring heaven here on earth; to bring light into darkness; to bring grace to bear upon nature; to *bring the city of God to the city of man.*'

Biblical text

Mk 5:18-20

'As Jesus was getting into the boat, the man who had been possessed with demons begged him that he might be with him. But he refused, and said to him, "Go home to your friends, and tell them how much the Lord has done for you, and how he had mercy on you". And he went away and began to proclaim in the Decapolis how much Jesus had done for him; and everyone marvelled.'

Homily

First of all let me say a word about the two personalities under consideration this evening; then we shall search in that passage from St Mark for some important elements; finally I shall suggest some points for meditation, for reflection on the values proposed by the biblical texts.

Giorgio La Pira and Pier Giorgio Frassati

The two personalities whose vocations I wish to reflect upon are Giorgio La Pira and, through his words, Pier Giorgio Frassati. I met La Pira only a few times, and in the context of meetings concerning Hebrew affairs. He had a great love for the Palestinian people and for the Arab world; but also for the Hebrew world and the State of Israel. I remember him best for the brightness of his eyes, for his smile, and his ability to communicate a sense of peace and joy. Using the words with which he himself described the young Frassati, I would say that he radiated purity, a supernatural clarity which allowed one a glimpse of an inner life, at the centre of which was contact with God. He is the example that will give us a grasp of our text from St Mark.

The other personality, Pier Giorgio Frassati, was already dead for several years when I began attending the same college in Turin where he had studied; but they still spoke of him. I like the idea of relating these two men by means of what one has written of the other, because jointly they have one single, important message to pass on to us, one which does not belong only to the past. We can think of them as living people still, even after their death, since both of them living in the power of the Resurrection of Christ care for our society today. They pray for us, with us they adore the Eucharist. Therefore as we prepare for the Eucharistic Congress, we ask the help of the witnesses to the faith in their own times and ours, that they would prepare us so that the Eucharist might effect its drawing power on us and on the contemporary world.

The Gospel text

We have read just the final part of the cure of the possessed man, because this is the part most relevant for our reflection.

When Jesus got out of the boat, the man he had cured begged to be allowed 'be with him.' It is firstly then a prayer: the man wanted to be with Jesus. In the original Greek text, the words are the same as those Mark used earlier at chapter 3, verse 14, in reporting how Jesus chose twelve 'to be with him.' This expression 'being with him' refers to the apostolic vocation, travelling around with Jesus and then being sent out in his name. It describes the call of the Twelve, that is the apostles, who continually share in the Master's ministry and are with him in the foundation of the Church.

What the cured man wanted was to belong to this group. But he received a hard answer, which echoes some other hard replies — like the one to the Canaanite woman which we have already seen. Mark the Evangelist says: 'He did not allow him'. Jesus did not want that man to be with him, that is to join those who left everything behind and journeyed around Palestine with him. The hardness of the reply is all the more evident if we set it alongside v.37 of the same chapter 5, when Jesus enters the house of Jairus and 'would not allow anyone to go with him except Peter, James and John.' Perhaps there were many who wanted to go into the house with him, perhaps out of curiosity; but he made a distinction: these three only, the others stay outside! The same Greek word used by Mark in both these cases of refusal is already found in Mark 1:35 where Jesus 'would not allow the demons to speak, because they knew him.'

Jesus sets up certain limits: this is not for you; it is not your vocation. It is a negative attitude to one who was mistaken about his vocation. We can imagine the disappointment of this man who, deeply grateful for his cure, wants to leave everything and follow Jesus in the same way as the chosen Twelve. But we should pay close attention to the words that follow the refusal. The man is told: 'Go home to your friends and tell them how much the Lord has done for you.' So he goes off to spread the good news about Jesus in the pagan region of Decapolis. These are words to ponder, since they convey the vocation of one who is not called like the Twelve, but nonetheless has a vocation to follow Jesus in the future building of the Church. He really shares in a calling. The Evangelist uses the significant word *'Go!'* It is some kind of missionary sending, a command to be a missionary.

What is his mission? To 'tell' and to 'proclaim.'.. both are characteristic terms for the evangelising work of the Church. Without being a missionary (or what we would nowadays call having a vocation of total dedication, involving the renunciation of house and family and trade), this man has a real and true mission of evangelisation. The *kerygma* is put in his mouth: 'tell, proclaim!'

What is he to tell? 'What the Lord has done for you, and how he showed mercy to you.' The message is closely linked to his own personality. He 'tells' by what is new in his own life, by his very manner of living, by the change that people see in him. Through this renewal he proclaims that his previous inability to communicate or work or make himself useful is now transformed into ability to do all these things.

There is one final significant point concerning this vocation: he is told, 'Go home to your friends'. And the Evangelist adds, 'he began to proclaim in the Decapolis'. It was not his calling to abandon all things — like Peter, James and the other apostles: he is sent home. In his own surroundings, in his own workplace, in the pagan societies and cities (Decapolis: ten cities) the Gerasene is sent forth to proclaim the mercy of God.

The lay vocation

We have thus described some characteristics of what may be called the *lay vocation*. In the story of salvation, there are vocations which are not (like those to priesthood and religious life) closely patterned on that of the Twelve, but are rather to be lived out in the everyday surroundings of home, work and society. They are, however, a true response to the command of Jesus, a true proclamation of the Kingdom.

This lay vocation in the Church was impressively lived by Giorgio La Pira and Pier Giorgio Frassati. Without abandoning their own state in life they took their proper place in it as living signs of God's mercy. Lay vocations are not simply 'missions' but they are a genuine way of holiness, which throughout history has formed many people who in moral, social, theological and supernatural virtues have been quite outstanding.

It is in this way that one can explain the fascination of La

Pira and Frassati; by the grace of God they are examples and forerunners of a huge multitude. And there are so many others! Some who are dead, but whom we once knew well: others who are still alive, and who know how to bring the power of God's Kingdom into every area of human activity.

That lovely passage from La Pira which we read at the beginning, and which I invite you to re-read and meditate again, flows from his deep intuition that every baptised person shares in a vocation. Apart from a life of radical self-giving which involves leaving behind house and family to follow Jesus, there are other effective ways of profound holiness, ways that are needed in order to fully express the potential of our baptism.

Questions for us

We too, you and I, are part of this great multitude of witnesses to Christ, called to witness the mercy of God. But each of us must listen to his own calling. Let me invite you to reflect on the central challenge posed by the text we have heard:

'How can you translate the ideal of fraternity, so central to the Christian faith, into social, political and economic structures if you take no practical interest in these structures — if you do not get involved in renewing and reforming whatever is outdated or wrong in these structures? How can you cause your Christian yeast to leaven the world — and so form a Christian civilisation and a Christian society — if you turn your back on social and political matters?'

Let me put this challenge in the form of three questions:

a) What have I thought about this point up to the present? What were my feelings and attitudes?

b) How have I acted in practice?

c) What is Jesus the Lord suggesting to me, as I kneel in adoration before him in the mystery of the Eucharist, since he wants to draw to himself not only my own life, but that of all the world?

We should ask Mary, to whom both Giorgio La Pira and Pier Giorgio Frassati were deeply devoted, to help us to listen to whatever Jesus wants to say to us. Let us ask her to make us ready to welcome his call, whatever it may be, and by our response become a means of salvation for many of our brothers.

7

CALLED TO BE ONE IN CHRIST

Seventh meeting, 2 June 1983

In this final meeting of our school of prayer for this year, we will consider a most important and fundamental vocation, one to which most people are called, namely the vocation to marriage. I think it will be good to hear what is said by this young couple who are engaged to be married in the near future.

The witness of an engaged couple

'We would just like to share our experience with you very simply and honestly. But from the start, we want to say that our vocation to marriage is a specific way of answering our baptismal calling to live as children of God.

A *first surprise* for us was the vitality of this vocation. It is not like the relationship between a master and his servant, of one in authority to those below. God calls but does not shout or command. So we have felt called to marriage by God's initiative; and yet at the same time we sense that in some unknown way he respects our full freedom. Our plan to marry is by God's guiding grace, and still it remains our own free decision.

When we look back on how our relationship has developed, it appears from one angle as a miracle — something willed and planned by God — while from the ordinary human point of view it can be explained as simply a free and unplanned mutual attraction, leading to our personal, spontaneous resolve. In our vocation as a couple — and, we believe, in every vocation — the wisdom of God somehow manages to combine the divine will and our human freedom.

A *second surprise* for us was the discovery that our vocation is not so much to *do* something but a calling to *become someone*. God is not a taskmaster. Among many examples in the Gospel, we can think of Zaccheus. After meeting the Lord and having become a 'new man' he had no need to wonder how he ought to behave. Rather it was immediately clear to him what he needed to do in order to live up to this new character he had become. Because his life was changed, his great works came straight from that.

So, we have stopped worrying about what should we do and instead focus on the question, what should we become? We are called to become love. Our existence together 'in the Lord' (and by 'in the Lord' Paul the apostle meant 'with the Lord') must speak to others about love.

To speak of love means to speak of God to others, because God is love. Our love for each other, though it is not a thing that can simply be forced to happen, can and must speak of God to others.

A friend of ours who is a priest explained it to us like this: 'God can find no more beautiful sign of *expressing himself* in this world than the love of a man and a woman.'

We believe that this is the major charism or 'talent' given to us, and that we must 'trade' with it rather than with any other. We are certain that the 'talent'of marriage is a special and irreplaceable ministry in the Church and one that can only be exercised by couples. Two people become one in Christ by the power of the Holy Spirit — that same Spirit which unites the Father and the Son and unites the Church to them. Married couples are meant to be a sign of this great mystery of love.

One idea was clear to us from the beginning, even though we discovered others as we went along: that a vocation as important as this cannot be just taken casually. It is something that has demanded our best energies and indeed, our whole existence. We have needed to give time to the 'couple', that it might give rise to a 'new person' who, is more than just the sum of the two of us. We feel it necessary to create a spirituality, that is a shared outlook that will stay with us along the various stages of life's journey together; one that will make room for the word of God and provide an answer to the problem of prayer; one that will characterise our affective and sexual life and help us opt for poverty; in a word, one that would fulfil our vocation as lay people, who are loyal children of the Church and truly in fellowship with all other people.

In a short while we will be married. Prudence and our lack of experience might suggest that we say nothing about this, but still we hope that the fruits of our engagment will mature in our married life. While the reality we are entering into is, of course, something wholly new to us, at the present time we are still making plans about the home life we hope to have — plans about openness with one another, hospitality, sobriety in the use of things and of money, plans about welcoming the children we hope to have, and the resolution to take up our lay vocation in its fullness. But the only sure prophecy we can make is that our marriage will surely carry forward the relationship we have had during our engagement and the journey that we have begun together.

More than anything else we have said, we would like to share this basic conviction: that marriage deeply lived in and with the Lord is a real way to holiness. It is a creative kind of union that has a message for others too, our brothers and sisters. For being called to this vocation, we are thankful to God the giver of all good and of all grace'.

Christine and Robert

Biblical text

John 2: 1-11.

'On the third day there was a marriage at Cana in Galilee and the mother of Jesus was there; Jesus also was invited to the marriage, with his disciples. When the wine ran short the mother of Jesus said to him ''They have no wine'', and Jesus said to her, ''Woman, what has that to do with me? My hour has not yet come.'' His mother said to the servants, ''Do whatever he tells you.'' Now six stone jars were standing there, for the Jewish rites of purification, each holding twenty or thirty gallons. Jesus said to them, ''Fill the jars with water''. And they filled them up to the brim. He said to them, ''Now draw some out, and take it to the steward of the feast.'' So they took it. When the steward tasted the water now become wine, and did not know where it had come from (though the servants who had drawn the water knew) he called the bridegroom and said to him, "Every man serves the good wine first and when they have drunk freely, then the poor wine; but you have kept the good wine until now." This, the first of his signs, Jesus did at Cana in Galilee and manifested his glory; and his disciples believed in him.'

Homily

We will try above all to reflect on our present situation.

This meditation is the first one after the Eucharistic Congress and the Pope's visit; and I believe we can see a connection between the School of Prayer that we have followed this year and that great school of popular prayer which so many people shared in during the Congress.

I feel that while we thank the Lord that the Congress succeeded so well in getting the people to pray, it was due in no small measure to yourselves and those meetings where for the past three years you have become accustomed to pray and to adore the mystery of God. The Holy Father was very taken by the spirit of prayer and worship he noticed in our people, in spite of the unfortunate weather conditions which made it all the more impressive that people chose to come and pray.

This evening our series of meetings for this year on the theme of 'Word-Eucharist-Vocation' comes to an end. We have looked at various kinds of vocation in the light of the Eucharist. By vocation we have meant not so much particular states of life but rather the *attitudes* which enter into all genuine search.

We have reflected upon the call to give one's life for one's brother using the example of **Maximilian Kolbe**; upon the typically contemplative call to suffer the dark night in the case of **St Thérèse of the Child Jesus**; on the call to be a brother to all, like **Charles de Foucauld**; on the vocation to a tireless, passionate search for truth even when that truth seems always just beyond our grasp, like **Simone Weil**; on the call to be involved in political action, like **Giorgio La Pira**.

But all these meditations up to now have focused on the call of individuals. Now we want to speak about a shared vocation where two people can say: 'This is *our* vocation, mine and yours together.' It is the vocation to marriage, a sign for every other kind of shared vocation.

Marriage is a sign of the Church, a sign of humanity called to be united to Christ, a sign of all men and all women called to be one. Indeed, through the mystery of two persons, a man and a woman joined into one, we see in miniature the vocation of the Church and of all humanity.

Scripture often speaks of this mystery, though frequently in parables and in dramatic or symbolic ways; and it would certainly be interesting to look at some pages of the Old Testament that tell of engagement, that is, at two people's search for their one shared vocation. I think of texts in Genesis about Isaac and Sarah, about Jacob and Rebecca. I think of the Book of Tobias, of Ruth and the Song of Songs. All of these could be read as a search by two people for a single vocation with the events that began it or obscured it, made it difficult, dramatic, exciting, marvellous, constructive or painful.

The wedding feast of Cana
Instead we have chosen just a New Testament episode from chapter 2 of the Gospel of St John: The Miracle at Cana.

At first sight the wedding seems to be a little in the background of the story; the wedding feast is mentioned but we are not given a clear picture of the young couple, we do not even hear their names! Only at the end do we catch a glimpse of the newly married husband and even then he appears as an improvident and ignorant man who is in the middle of a situation whose meaning he does not fully understand.

But, in truth, this story told by St John, like all others in his Gospel, is a very rich mystery; so I invite you to read it again in order to get a little beyond the external facts and grasp some of the varied meaning it has for our present interest.

To help us in this let us pray to Mary who plays a central part in this mystery: 'O Mary, Mother of Jesus, let us understand the mystery of the vocation to love which is hidden behind these lines, and behind the living power of this passage of the Gospel.

May we grasp the meaning of the words that were spoken without undervaluing or exaggerating them but tasting their true value'.

Let me draw your attention especially to three statements in the story: *the opening one*, 'On the third day there was a wedding in Cana and the Mother of Jesus was there'; the *central one*, Mary's statement 'they have no wine'; and the Evangelist's *final comment* that 'Jesus manifested his glory', that is, in this miracle performed at a wedding.

The mystery of the third day

We begin with the first of these, the mysterious reference to the third day. John, who is never haphazard in the way he tells his story, introduces this episode — the first in a series of miracles, and of the manifestations of his glory — by mentioning the third day.

What can this third day mean? John's first two chapters describe an intense week of events, calculated day by day, up to this, the third day. In chapter 1 we can easily deduce the opening days of the ministry of Jesus. Verse 28 mentions the *first day*, when John the Baptist proclaims the presence of one greater than himself. Next, the Evangelist mentions 'the following day', that is the *second*, when Jesus comes on the scene and is called the Lamb of God. On the day after, which *ought to be* the third day, he meets the two disciples and says to them, 'Come and see' and the disciples remain with him all that day, from the tenth hour.

On the following day still, which really should count as the *fourth* day, Jesus goes towards Galilee and meets Philip and Nathanael. At this point the evangelist says, 'on the third day there was a marriage at Cana in Galilee.' But if we recall how in the Bible the phrase 'the third day' can often mean *'two days later'*, (counting the first as one of three) we would actually arrive at placing the Cana episode on the *sixth* day of that great week, which is the day of *the creation of man and woman*.

St John — who begins his Gospel with the opening words of *Genesis*: 'In the beginning...' — deliberately shows us an entire week of events (parallel to the Creation story). The sixth day then is the one when, in the mystery of a man and a woman uniting their lives in marriage at Cana in Galilee, Jesus manifests his glory.

One might say that the Evangelist portrays this week to correspond to the first week of creation, with the deliberate intent of making the episode at Cana correspond to the moment when God created man in his own image and likeness, and created woman to be his companion. Through this chronological symbolism St John seems to say that the sign performed by Jesus on this day is the continuation and climax of God's creative work on behalf of the couple.

But on the other hand, Jesus' intervention arose because he noticed the needs found in the situation of the man, his wife and their union: 'They have no wine.'

The whole of the fourth Gospel indeed draws out the links that run through the entire story of salvation. Towards the end of St John's Gospel, we find another period of six days; and the sixth is the day on which Jesus dies upon the cross, with the Woman, Mary his mother, standing beside him. There Jesus restores man — the beloved disciple — to his fullness. The cross manifests fully the glory of God which only began to be manifested in that first miracle at Cana. At the wedding feast, the glory was shown in an initial and partial way; yet it gives some idea of the love with which God draws near to the human situation, to deal with its intimate needs and bring it to its fullness and true joy.

Inability to love

Within the background we have sketched out, what meaning should we give to Mary's statement, 'They have no wine'? There are some other expressions like this elsewhere in the Gospels. One that springs to mind is the complaint, 'We have no more oil, our lamps are going out' *(Mt 25:8)* — which conveys a similar situation of need and improvidence on the occasion of a marriage feast. Another example would be the situation of the crowd which followed Jesus into the desert; the disciples had no idea how to provide food for all these people *(Jn 6: 9)*.

There are times when we find ourselves wanting, unable to cope with a situation; we are responsible for a need which is in stark contrast with the atmosphere of festivity, joy and expectancy, with the hope of unfading love. Just at the point when one might expect that the fullness of love at the marriage feast, that standing together listening to the Word, would lead to happiness ever after... just at that moment, we find improvidence, human provisions that are inadequate, the resources that run out, and little prudence. There follows a need which traps them; the man and the woman cannot know what to do.

This marriage feast seems about to end in disappointment, in a nightmare of ill-fortune. Ever afterwards this pair would be remembered as having bad luck, as incapable of planning properly for their own wedding feast, let alone of running a home well.

We now see the profound meaning of the cry, 'They have no wine.' The man and the woman, created in order to form together a perfect unity, have not got enough wine for the sixth day — the day of their union, the day for the foundation of the family, at work and the building of society — which should precede the seventh day, the day of rest.

The man and woman go through an experience of frustration, of incapacity. They had counted entirely on their mutual understanding, on their being called to be one. And this vocation, their marriage feast, comes under threat because of their imprudence, lack of foresight, human weakness of various kinds. To broaden this idea further, though the man and woman feel themselves called to love and know this is a real vocation which they cannot do without, yet still in some profound sense they feel unable to *love*.

Admittedly, not everyone has the courage to make this admission, which is so deep and so radical. People prefer to blame the failure of their love on misunderstanding, ambiguity, nervousness, opposition, weariness, incompatibility or the boredom of daily life. It is perhaps rare for a man or woman to face up to this painful question: 'Am I really capable of loving?' Yet this is the most vital question in the whole of human existence: the human person, each one of us, is called to love; but are we really able to love? Are our reserves of love and

67

patience — like our supplies of wine and oil and bread — sufficient to support us for a lifetime? Or are we inclined to admit: 'I do not want to go on; my lamp has gone out'? This can happen within any vocation which includes the choice of unity, of daily service and of sacrifice. But at such moments, perhaps we have someone close to us, like Mary, who understands our situation and says 'They have no more wine!' — someone who helps, when our resources have run out.

The transforming power of the Eucharist

The final statement, 'There Jesus manifested his glory', gives us the message of this Gospel text which has led us into the heart of a human situation which is both frequent and dramatic.

The Eucharist is the transformation of water into wine, of human fragility into energy and wisdom. It is a gift of the Spirit who alone can give us certainty that we are capable of love.

The Eucharist is the power that nourishes every form of love which truly unites: the love that unites an engaged couple, the love that unites the couple in marriage, the love that can bind us into community, into Church, into society. The Eucharist is the manifestation of the powerful glory of God. The man whose wine has run out, who finds himself left with nothing but tasteless and colourless water, needs the fullness of that new Spirit which will transform his heart and mind. Only then can he rely upon the kind of love that is not just short-lived enthusiasm, half-baked plans and shallow experiences but which will be a reliable basis for the whole of his life.

This is why at the end of all our reflections for this year we come back again to the Eucharist as Jesus who, drawing all to himself from the cross, gives to man, to woman, to all humanity, the ability to be themselves.

So we can say to him: 'We thank you Lord for giving us the power to be ourselves in the truth of our calling which you continually renew within us by the power of your Eucharist.' And since tomorrow is the twentieth anniversary of the death of Pope John XXIII let us also thank the Lord for strengthening this man through the Eucharist to be himself in his humble and great vocation to the world. We pray also for John Paul II, who was recently here with us in this Cathedral to worship the Eucharist, that the Lord may grant to him and to us the power to be ourselves in an authentic response to our vocation.

Some final questions for ourselves
During the period of silence that will follow now we could ask ourselves how we could re-live in this coming summer the experience of the Eucharist Congress and the power of the Eucharist which we have experienced. For example we might ask:

a) How I might share my love and appreciation for the Eucharist with those whom I meet.

b) How to profit from the holiday period courageously and wisely, to find suitable and frequent occasions for silence and adoration.

c) What practical steps I might take so that what has been planted in my heart during our school of prayer can yield its fruit and come to maturity.